NATURE (speaks).

GOOD heavens, how deeply I am often saddened at seeing the human race, which God created perfect, in His own image, and appointed to be the lords of the earth, depart so far away from me! I allude more particularly to you, O stolid philosophaster, who presume to style yourself a practical chemist, a good philosopher, and yet are entirely destitute of all knowledge of me, of the true Matter, and of the whole Art which you profess! For, behold, you break vials, and consume coals, only to soften your brain still more with the vapours. You also digest alum, salt, orpiment, and atrament; you melt metals, build small and large furnaces, and use many vessels: nevertheless, I am sick of your folly, and you suffocate me with your sulphurous smoke. With most intense heat you seek to fix your quicksilver, which is the vulgar volatile substance, and not that out of which I make metals; therefore you effect nothing. For you do not follow my guidance, or strive to imitate my methods, rather mistaking my whole artifice. You would do better to mind your own business, than to dissolve and distil so many absurd substances, and then to pass them through alembics, cucurbitas, stills, and pelicans. By this method you will never succeed in congealing quicksilver. For the revivification you use a reverberatory fire, and make it so hot as to render everything liquid—thus do you finish your work, and in the end ruin yourself and others. You will never discover anything unless you first enter my workshop, where, in the inmost bowels of the earth I ceaselessly forge metals: there you may find the substance which I use, and discover the method of my work.

Do not suppose that I will reveal my secret to you unless you first find the growing seed of all metals (resembling that of the animals and vegetables). I preserve in the bosom of the earth both that which is used for their generation, and that with which they are nourished up.

Metals *Exist*, vegetables *Live and Grow*, and animals *Feel*, which is more than merely to grow.

A DEMONSTRATION OF NATURE,

MADE TO THE ERRING ALCHEMISTS, AND COMPLAINING OF THE SOPHISTS AND OTHER FALSE TEACHERS.

SET FORTH BY
JOHN A. MEHUNG.

I make metals, stones, and the atramental substances out of certain elements, which I mix and compound in a certain way. These elements you must seek in the heart of the earth, and nowhere else. Vegetables contain their own seed, and image; in like manner, animals are propagated, and by the same means do generate their own likeness. Everything proceeds by the laws laid down for it. Only you, wicked man, who try to usurp my office, have departed further from me than any other creature. Metals have no life, or principle of generation and growth, if they lack their own proper seed. The first is accomplished by the four elements in nine days; the Moon goes through the twelve heavenly signs in twenty-nine and a half days.

By the aforesaid laws, winter and summer relieve each other, the elements are changed, generations take place in the earth—through my working, through the working of God and the heavens, do all things subsist, the perceptible, the visible, and the invisible. Thus all things in heaven which are comprehended under the Moon, do work, and impart their influence to the substance, which, like a woman, longs to conceive seed. Each star influences its own substance, and according to their peculiar nature, they produce different things. They work first in heaven above, then in the earth beneath in the elements, each according to its own peculiar virtue; and hence arise species and individual things.

You are to know that these manifold influences do not pour themselves fruitlessly upon the earthly elements. For though their working is invisible, yet it is a most certain and real thing. The earth is surrounded by heaven, and from it obtains her best influences and substances. Every sphere is ready to communicate its truth, and therewith to pervade her centre. Through this motion and heat, there arise upon earth vapours, which are the first substances. If the vapour is cold and moist, it sinks down again to the earth, and is there preserved; that which is moist and warm ascends to the clouds. That which is shut up in the earth I change, after a long time, into the substance of sulphur, which is the active, and into quicksilver, which is the passive principle. The metals are another mixture of this first composition. The whole is obtained from the four elements, which I form into one mass. This process I repeat so often that you have no excuse for a mistake.

After the putrefaction comes the generation, which is brought about by the internal incombustible warmth heating the coldness of the quicksilver, which gladly submits to this heat because it wishes to be united to its sulphur. All these things, fire, air, and water, I have in one alembic in the earth. There I digest, dissolve, and sublime them, without any hammer, tongs, file, coals, vapour, fire, "bath of S. Mary," or other sophisticated contrivances. For I have my own heavenly fire which excites the elemental according as the matter desires to put on a suitable and comely form. Thus I extract my quicksilver from the four elements, or their substance. This is always accompanied by its sulphur, which is its second self, and warms it gradually, gently, and pleasantly. Thus the cold becomes warm, and the dry moist and oily. But the moist is not without its dry substance, nor is the dry without its moist: one is conserved by the other in its first essence (which is the elementary spirit of the essence, or the quintessence) from which proceeds the generation of our child. The fire brings it forth, and nourishes it in the air, but before that, it is decomposed in virgin earth; then water flows forth (or it flows forth from the water), which we must seek, since it is my first Matter, and the source of my mineral. For contrary resists strenuously to contrary, and doth in such wise fortify itself, lest perchance it be carried away in operating; then does it suffer transmutation, and is stripped of its form by the concupiscence of matter, which incessantly attracts a new form.

By my wisdom I govern the first principle of motion. My hands are the eighth sphere, as my Father ordained; my hammers are the seven planets, with which I forge beautiful things. The substance out of which I fashion all my works, and all things under heaven, I obtain from the four elements alone. Chaos, or Hyle, is the first substance. This is the Mistress that maintains the King, the Queen, and the whole court. A horseman is always ready to do her bidding, and a virgin performs her office in the chambers. The more beautiful she is, the more beautiful do I appear in her. Know also that I have power to give their essence to all essences, that it is I who preserve them, and mould them into shape. Moreover, observe the three parts into which God has divided the first substance. Of the first and purest part He created the Cherubin, Seraphin, Archangels, and all the other angels. Out of the second, which was not so pure, He created the heavens and all that belongs to them; of the third, impure part, the elements and their properties. First and best of these is *Fire*. Fire admits of no corruption, and contains the purest part of the quintessence. After *Fire*, He made the subtle Air, and put into it a part (but not so large a part) of the quintessence. Then came the visible element of Water, which has as much of the quintessence as it needs. Last of all comes the *Earth*. All these (like all the rest of Nature) He created in a moment of time. The earth is gross and dark, and though it is fruitful, yet it contains the smallest part of the quintessence. At first the elements remained as they were in their separate spheres. So Air is really moist, but is properly tempered by Fire. Water is really warm, but obtains its moisture from the air. The Earth is really dry, but it is also cold; its great dryness renders it akin to fire. Fire, however, is the first of elements which causes life and growth by its heat.

Now all these elements influence and qualify each other, so that each in its turn is now active, now passive. For instance, Fire works upon air and earth. Earth is the mother and nurse of all things, and sustains all that is liable to decay under heaven. Now God has given me power to resolve the four elements into their quintessence; this is that first substance which in every element is generically qualified. I resolve them for my own purpose, and thereby bring about all generation. But no one will be able to resolve me into my first substance, as he strives to resolve the elements. For I alone can transmute the elements and their forms, and he who thinks otherwise deceives himself. For you will never be able to assign to each substance its proper influence, or to find the correct proportions of the elements which are required by that substance. I alone, I say, can form created things, and give to them their peculiar properties and substance. By my heavenly mysteries I produce perfect works, which are justly called miracles, as may be seen in the Elixir which has such marvellous virtue, and is of my own forming. No art upon earth can add anything to, or improve upon, my workmanship. Every sane person must see that nothing can be accomplished without a perfect knowledge of the heavenly bodies, or apart from the efficacy which abides in them; without these everything is error and misuse; and yet, whence is a mere man to obtain this influence, and how is he to apply it to the substance? How can he mingle the elements in their right proportions? Even if a man were to spend a long life in the investigation of this secret (says Avicenna, De Vir. Cord., cp. ii.), he would not get any nearer to its solution. It is entrusted to my keeping alone, and can never be known to any man. By my virtue and efficacy I make the imperfect perfect, whether it be a metal or a human body. I mix its ingredients, and temper the four elements. I reconcile opposites, and calm their discord.

This is the golden chain which I have linked together of my heavenly virtues and earthly substances. I accomplish my works with such unerring accuracy that in them all my power is shewn forth, and with so much skill that the wisest of men cannot attain to my perfection. Go forth then, and behold my works, you who think yourself so skilled a workman, and (without any knowledge of me), with your coal fires and your S. Mary's bath, strive to make gold potable in my alembics—and know that I cannot bear the sight of your folly. Are you not ashamed, after considering my works, to attempt to rival them with your malodorous decoctions in your coloured and painted vials, and thus lose both your time and your money? I am at a loss to conceive what you can be thinking. Have pity upon yourself, and consider my teaching. Try to understand rightly what I tell you, for I cannot lie. Consider how that most glorious metal, gold, has received its beautiful form from heaven and its precious substance from the earth. The generation of the precious stones, such as carbuncles, amethysts, and diamonds, takes place in the same manner. The substance itself is composed of the four elements; its form and qualities it receives through heavenly influences, although the capacity of being thus wrought upon slumbers in the element and is only brought out and purified in the course of time. All this is accomplished by my hands alone. I am the architect, and no one else knows the secret of life. For, however wise he may think himself, he does not know how much to take of each element, or where to obtain it, or how to mingle hostile elements so as to allay their discord, or how to bring the heavenly influences to bear on these essences. He cannot even make iron, or lead, or the very basest of metal; how then should he be able to make gold except by stealing my treasure? The object which he desires can be accomplished by my art alone—an art which it is impossible for man to know.

And even though we allow gold to be the most precious of metals, yet gold by itself cannot cure diseases, or heal the imperfections of other metals, or change them into gold. In the same way glass (which might otherwise be the Philosopher's Stone) can never become so soft as to be rendered malleable. Gold alone is the most precious and the most perfect of all the metals. But if you cannot even make lead, or the minutest grain of any metals, or produce the fruit of any herb, how hopeless must your search after the art of making gold appear! Again if you say that you wish to produce some chemical result, even if it do not turn out to be gold, I answer that you thereby only give a fresh proof of your folly. Can you not understand that the secret of my innermost working must always remain a sealed book to you? What Nature does can never be successfully imitated by any created being. Nay, if I made gold out of seven metals, and you do not understand my method, how can you ever hope to prepare the substance which itself changes all metals into the purest gold, and is the most precious treasure that God has given me? You are foolish and ignorant, if you do not know that this precious thing which you seek is, to the created mind, the greatest mystery of Nature, and that it is compounded by heavenly influences— and thus has power to heal and deliver men from all diseases, and to remove the imperfection of the base metals. If, therefore, it is in itself so perfect that it has not its like upon earth, it must surely be the workmanship of the highest Intelligence, since no one else can even make gold, and certainly not produce a thing which has itself the power of making gold. Surely, to maintain that you are able to prepare such a thing, is like saying that you cannot carry ten pounds, but that you are strong enough to carry a hundred pounds. Put to heart, therefore, the true scope and responsibility of your intent.

I, myself, again, receive all my wisdom, virtue, and power from heaven, and my Matter, in its simplest form, is the four elements. This is the first principle and the quintessence of the elements, which I bring forth by reductions, time, and circulations, by which I transmute the inferior into the more perfect, the cold and dry into the moist and warm; and thus I preserve stones and metals in their natural state of moisture. This is brought about by the movements of the celestial bodies, for by them the elements are ruled; by their controlling influence like is brought to like. The purer my substance is, the more excellent are the results produced by the heavenly influence. And do you think that there in your alembic, where you have your earth and water, I will be induced by your fire and heat, and by your white and red colour, to bend my neck to your yoke, and to do your will and pleasure? Do you think that you can move the heavens, and force them to shed their influence upon your work. Do you think that that is an organic instrument which gives forth sweet music only when it is touched by the musician's fingers? You take too much upon yourself, you foolish man. Do you not know that the revolutions of the heavens are governed by a mighty Mind, which, by its influence, imparts power to all things?

I beseech you to remember that all great things proceed from me, and, in the last instance, from God; and not to suppose that the skill of your hands can be as perfect as the operation of Nature. For it is void and vain, and, ape-like, must imitate me in all things. Nor must you suppose that your distilling, dissolving, and condensing of your substance in your vessel, or your eliciting of water out of oil, is the right way of following me. Far from it, my son. All your mixing and dissolving of elements never has produced, and never can produce, any good result. Do you wish to know the reason? Your substance cannot stand the heat of the furnace for a single half-hour, but must evaporate in smoke, or be consumed by the fire. But the substance with which I work, can stand any degree of heat, without being injured. My water is dry, and does not moisten what it touches; it does not evaporate, or become less, neither is its oil consumed. So perfect are my elements; but yours are worse than useless.

In conclusion, let me tell you that your artificial fire will never impart my heavenly warmth, nor will your water, oil, and earth supply you with any substitute for my substance. It is the gift of God, shed upon the elements from heaven, and upon one more than upon another; but how, is known only to me, and to the Great Artist who entrusted me with this knowledge. One thing more let me tell you, my son. If you would imitate me, you must prepare all out of one simple, self-contained Matter, in *one* well-closed vessel, and in *one* alembic. The substance contains all that is needed for its perfect development, and must be prepared with a warmth that is always kept at the same gentle temperature. Let me ask you to consider the birth and development of man, my noblest work. You cannot make a human body out of any substance whatsoever. Of my method in forming so subtle a body neither Aristotle nor Plato had the remotest knowledge. I harden the bones and the teeth, I make the flesh soft, the muscles cold, the brain moist, the heart, into which God has poured the life, warm, and fill all the veins with red blood. And in the same way, I make of one quicksilver, and of one active male sulphur, one maternal vessel, the womb of which is the alembic. It is true that man aids me with his art, by shedding external heat into the matrix; more than this, however, he cannot do. He, then, that knows the true Matter, and prepares it properly in a well-closed vessel, and puts the whole in an alembic, and keeps up the fire at the proper degree of warmth, may safely leave the rest to me. Upon the fire all depends, and much, therefore, does it behove you to see thereto. Consider, therefore, the fire, which they call epesin, pepsin, pepausin, and optesin, or natural, preternatural, and infranatural fire, which burns not. Without the true Matter and the proper fire, no one can attain the end of his labour. I give you the substance; you must provide the mere outward conditions. Take, then, a vessel, and an alembic of the right kind and of the right size. Be wise, and perform the experiment in accordance with my laws. Help me, and I will help you. I will deal with you as you deal with me. To my other sons, who have treated me well, have obeyed their father and mother, and submitted themselves to my precepts, I have given a great reward, as John de Mehung, for instance, will tell you. His testimony is also borne out by Villanova, Raymond, Morienus the Roman, Hermes (whom they call Father, and who has not his like among the Sages), Geber, and others who have written about this Art, and know by experience that it is true.

If you, my son, wish to prepare this precious Stone, you need not put yourself to any great expense. All that you want is leisure, and some place where you can be without any fear of interruption. Reduce the Matter which is *one*), to powder, put it, together with its water, in a well-closed vessel, and expose it to continuous, gentle heat, which will then begin to operate, while the moisture favours the decomposition. The presence of the moisture prevents the dryness of the quicksilver from retarding its assimilation.

Meanwhile, you must diligently observe what I do, and remember the words of Aristotle (Meteor iii. and iv.), who says: Study Nature, and carefully peruse the book concerning Generation and Corruption." You must also read the book concerning heaven and the world, in which you will find indicated the beautiful and pure substance. If you neglect this study, you will fail. On this subject consult Albertus Magnus, De Mineralibus. But if your eyes are opened by such studies, you will discover the secret of the growth of minerals, viz., that they are all produced from the elements.

First learn to know *me*, before you call yourself Master. Follow me, that am the mother of all things created, which have one essence, and which can neither grow, nor receive a living soul, without the heavenly and elementary influences. When you have learned by persevering study to understand the virtues of the heavenly bodies, their potent operations, and the passive condition of the elements, and its reason—if you further know the media of transmutation, the cause of generation, nutrition, and decay, and the essence and substance of the elements—you are already acquainted with the Art, notwithstanding that a most subtle mind is still needed for the studying of my operations. But if you do not possess part at least of this knowledge, you will be fortunate indeed if you succeed in discovering my secret. It is a secret that is read not by those that are wise in their own conceits, but by those that humbly and patiently listen to my teaching. Therefore, if you desire to own this treasure, which has been the reward of the truly wise in all ages, you must do as I bid you. For my treasure has such virtue and potency that the like of it is to be found neither in heaven nor upon earth. It holds an intermediate position between Mercury and the Metal which I take for the purpose of extracting from it by your art and my knowledge that most precious essence. It is pure and potable gold, and its radical principle is active humidity. Moreover, it is the universal Medicine described by Solomon (Eccles. xxxviii.); the same also is taken from the earth, and honoured by the wise. God has assigned it a place among my mysteries, and reveals it to the Sages, although many who call themselves learned doctors of Theology and Philosophy, hold it in ignorant contempt—as Alchemy is also despised by the doctors of Medicine, because they do not know me, and are ignorant of that which they profess to teach. They must be insufficiently furnished with brains, or they would not direct their foolish scorn against the panacea which renders all other medicines unnecessary. Happy is the man, even though he be sinking under the weight of years, whose days God prolongs until he has come to the knowledge of this secret! For (as Geber says) many to whom this gift was imparted late in life, have, nevertheless, been refreshed and delighted by it in extreme old age.

He that has this secret possesses all good things and great riches. One ounce of it will ensure to him both wealth and health. It is the only source of strength and recreation, and far excels the golden tincture. It is the elixir and water of life, which includes all other things. In my treasure are concealed quicksilver, sulphur, incombustible oil, white, indestructible, and fusible salt. I tell you, frankly, that you will never be able to accomplish its preparation without me, just as I can do nothing without your help. But if you understand my teaching, and cooperate with me, you can accomplish the whole thing in a short time.

Have done with the charlatans, and their foolish writings; have done with all their various alembics, and phials; have done with their excrements of horses, and all the variety of their coal-fires, since all these things are of no use whatever. Do not perplex yourself with metals, or other things of a like nature: rather change the elements into a mutable form. For this is the most excellent substance of the Sages, and is rejected only by the foolish. Its substance is like, but its essence unlike, that of gold. Transmute the elements and you will have what you seek. Sublime that which is the lowest, and make that which is the highest, the lowest. Take quicksilver which is mixed with its active sulphur; put it into a well-closed vial, and one alembic, plunge one-third of it into the earth, kindle the fire of the Sages, and watch it well so that there may be no smoke. The rest you may leave to me. I ask you to do no more, but only bid you follow my unerring guidance.

THE ANSWER OF THE CHEMIST,

In which he confesses his errors, asks pardon for them, and returns thanks to Nature.

Dearest Mother Nature, who, next to the angels, art the most perfect of all God's creatures, I thank thee for thy kindly instruction. I acknowledge and confess that thou art the Mother and Empress of the great world, made for the little world of man's mind. Thou movest the bodies above, and transmutest the elements below. At the bidding of thy Lord thou dost accomplish both small things and great, and renewest, by ceaseless decay and generation, the face of the earth and of the heavens. I confess that nothing can live without a soul, and that all that exists and is endued with being flows forth from thee by virtue of the power that God has given to thee. All matter is ruled by thee, and the elements are under thy governance. From them thou takest the first substance, and from the heavens thou dost obtain the form. That substance is formless and void until it is modified and individualized by thee. First thou givest it a substantial, and then an individual form. In thy great wisdom thou dost cunningly mould all thy works through the heavenly influences, so that no mortal hand can utterly destroy them. Under thy hands God has put all things that are necessary to man, and through thee, He has divided them into four kingdoms, namely, those that have being and essence, like the metals and stones; those that have essence and growth, like the vegetables; those that have feeling and sensation, like the beasts, birds, and fishes. These are the first three classes; in the fourth it pleased God to place only the noblest and most perfect of His works, namely, man, to whom He also gave a rational and immortal soul. This soul is obscured by the defilement which found its way into the body through the senses, and, but for the grace and mercy of God, would have become involved in its condemnation. Hence the chief perfection of man is not derived from thee, nor dost thou impart to us our humanity. Nevertheless, the material part of man is the work of thy hands alone.

And, surely, our bodies are cunningly and wonderfully made, and, in every part of them, bear witness to the masterly skill of the workman. How marvellous are the uses of our various members! How wonderful that the soul can move them and set them to work at will! But, alas! oftener still the body is master of the soul, and forces it to do many things which pure reason condemns. If we consider the matter from this point of view, it seems as though thou hadst begun well, and yet thy work had, after all, turned out an abortion. Wert thou wanting in wisdom, or knowledge, or couldst thou not do otherwise? Pardon me if I speak too presumptuously about thy wisdom, I only desire to be rightly and truly informed. For, indeed, even now thy stern rebuke has made many things clear to me. I have spent my whole life in attending to thy lessons; and the more closely I have listened, the more clearly have I understood my mistakes and the depth of thy wisdom. Now, whether I lie, or stand, or walk, I can think of nothing but thy great mystery. And yet I am unable to conceive what substance and form I must take for it. Thou didst sternly rebuke me for not following thy way; but thou knowest that, if I do not obey thee, it is only because I do not know what thou wouldst have me do. I shall' never be able to attain any satisfactory result in this Art, unless thou wilt enlighten my blindness. Thou hast rightly said that it is not for man to know the mystery of thy working: how then can I be guided to this knowledge, unless thou wilt take me by the hand? Thou sayest that I must follow thee; and I am willing to do so. But tell me what I must do, and what books I must study for that purpose. Of the books which I have read, one says, "Do this," and the other, "No, do that "; and they are full of unintelligible expressions and of dark parables. At last I see that I cannot learn anything from them. Therefore I take refuge with thee, and instantly beseech thee to advise and to tell me how to set about this difficult task. On my knees I implore thee to show me the way by which I can penetrate into the lower parts of the earth, and by what subtle process I am to obtain the' perfect mercury of the metals. And yet I doubt whether any man, even after obtaining this mercury, can really make gold. That is thy work, and not the work of man; as thy words and my own experience most clearly shew.

We see that the cold and moist mercury needs the assistance of its sulphur, which is its seed after its kind, or its homogeneous sperm, out of which the metal or Stone must be produced. But thou sayest only: Take the proper substance, the proper vessel, the proper mineral, the proper place, and the proper fire; then form, colour, and life will grow and spring forth from thence. Thou art the Architect; thou knowest the glorious properties of the Matter. The active principle can do nothing unless there be a passive principle prepared to receive its influence. Thou knowest how to mix the warm and the cold, the dry and the moist; by reconciling hostile elements, thou canst produce new substances and forms. For I did indeed understand all that thou didst tell me, but am unable to express it so well as thou. This thou hast firmly impressed on my mind, that the Elixir is composed by the reconciling and mutual transmutation of the four elements. But what man is sufficient for such a task? For who knows how earth can have its essence in common with air, or how it can be changed into moisture which is contrary to its nature? For humidity will not leave a cold and humid element, not even under the influence of fire. This, too, is the work of Nature, that it becomes black, and white, and red. These three visible colours correspond to the three elements, earth, water, and fire, and are pervaded by the air. Then, again, thou sayest that the Stone is prepared of one thing, of one substance, in one vessel, the four (elements) composing one essence in which is one agent which begins and completes the work; man, thou sayest, need do nothing but add a little heat, and leave the rest to thy wisdom. For all that is needed is already contained in the substance, in perfection, beginning, middle, and end, as the whole man, the whole animal, the whole flower is contained each in its proper seed. Now, in the human seed the human specific-substance is also included, as flesh, blood, hair, &c.; and thus every seed contains all the peculiar properties of its species. In the whole world men spring from human seed, plants from plants, animals from animals. Now I know that when once the seed is enclosed in the female vessel, no further trouble or work of any kind is required—everything is brought to perfection by thy gradual and silent working. And the generation of the Stone, thou sayest, is performed in a similar manner. Only one substance is required, which contains within itself air, water, and fire—in short, everything that is needed for the completion of this work. No further handling of any kind is necessary, and a gentle fire is sufficient to rouse the internal warmth, just as an infant in the womb is cherished by natural heat. The only thing in which man must aid thee, is, by preparing the substance, removing all that is superfluous, enclosing this simple earth, which is combined with its water, in a vessel, and subjecting it to the action of gentle heat in a suitable alembic. This, thou sayest, is all that needs to be done by man; when all has been prepared for thee, thou dost begin thy part of the work. Thou dissolvest the substance, and makest the dry watery; then thou sublimest it, and bearest it upward into the air, and thus, without any further aid, bringest that to perfection which can itself impart perfection to all imperfect things. Therefore, thou, Nature, art the first mother, since thou dost cunningly combine the four elements into an essence by a process of which none but thou has any knowledge. Thus far have I understood thee, and do not quite despair, if it be pleasing unto God and to thee, of seeing thy great reward with my own eyes.

But at present I earnestly desire to know but one thing: and that is, how can that substance be obtained, what are its qualities, and what its powers to impart perfection to imperfect things?

I am well aware that gold is the most precious of the metals; but I cannot see that it has any capacity of becoming more potent than it already is. For whatever man may do with it, it will never be able to perfect anything but itself. If any one told me to dissolve it and extract from it its quicksilver, I should regard that as a very foolish direction; for nothing can be got out of gold but what is in it. These philosophasters betray their ignorance by saying that they can reduce gold to its first substance; but thy instruction has made it clear to me that the first substance cannot be obtained, except by destroying the specific properties of a thing, nor can any new species be brought forth by such a destruction, unless the species be first universalized into the genus. Moreover, I make bold to affirm that no man can first resolve gold into its generic substance, and then restore it again; for when it has once lost its specific properties, no mere human skill can change it back into what it was before. Nor can any one really reduce gold to the first form imparted to it by the elements. For gold is not transmuted either by heat or by cold, and is so perfect in its kind that fire only renders it purer. It does not admit of any further development, and therefore no other metal or quicksilver can be obtained from it.

It is true that plants and animals are constantly producing their like by means of their seed, and their capacity of organic nutrition. But I do not see how the same can be said of metals, seeing that at the expiration of any given period they still retain the same size and weight which they had at the beginning. Through thee they receive their being out of the elements without any sowing, planting, or development of any kind. Moreover, I know that no credit is to be attached to the fanciful notions of the old Sages who would prepare our Stone out of a crude metallic substance, and do not understand that the form and substance of a thing are conditioned by its essential nature. Now, I remember a certain juggling charlatan, who was looked upon as a great philosopher, telling me that the only true material was common quicksilver, which must be well mingled with gold, since in such an union the one brought the other to perfection. If I did this, continued that impostor, I should be able to prepare the Elixir. First, however, the four elements must be separated from each other, then, after each had been purified, they must be reunited, the great being combined with the small, and the subtile with the gross. This, he said, was the right way of making the Stone. But I know that all this is sheer nonsense, and that such men are only deceiving themselves and others.

I am also aware that only God can produce anything out of the elements. He alone knows how to mingle and combine them in their due proportions. For He alone is the Creator and Author of all good things, and there is nothing in the world that He has not made. Therefore, let the charlatans cease their vainglorious talk, and remember that they can never hope to gather where they cannot sow; let them make an end of their false calcinations, sublimations, distillations, by which they extract the spirit in a vaporous form, and of their juggling coagulations and congelations, by which they pretend, even among the initiated, to be able rightly to separate the elements of gold and quicksilver. It is certainly true that all things under heaven are composed of the four elements, and mixed of them according to the due proportion of their genus and species; but it is not simply the union of the four elements, but their being combined in a certain way, which constitutes the substance of the Philosophical Stone.

I also understand that in the red quicksilver and perfect body, which is called the Sun, the four elements are combined in a peculiar way, and so inseparably conjoined, that no mere human art can divide them. For all ancient and true Sages say that fire and air are enclosed in earth and water, and contend so violently with each other that none but God and Nature can loosen their grappling embrace. This I can truly affirm and also prove. For we can neither see the fire nor grasp the air; and if any one says that the several elements can be seen he is an imposter, seeing that they are inseparably and inextricably conjoined. For, although the Sophists pretend, and confidently affirm, that they can divide gold and quicksilver into the four elements, yet for all that they speak not the truth. If two elements, fire and air, were thus taken away, all the rest must vanish into nothing. They may say that those two are retained, but they are, nevertheless, densely ignorant as to what becomes of them; for air and fire cannot be seen or perceived. Again, that extract which they call fire and air renders humid, which is not the property either of fire or of air.

Moreover, as thou hast said, even the most learned Doctor cannot know the proportion of each element in any given substance. For God has entrusted this knowledge to thee alone. Nor is any Sage wise enough to be able to mingle and put together the elements so as to produce any natural object. If then he dissolves anything into its elements, how, I pray thee, is he to put them together again into any abiding form, since he is ignorant of their proportionate quantity and quality, and of the method of their composition? Yet it is of no use to separate them, if they cannot be put together again. To thee, O Nature, we must entrust this task, since thou knowest the art of preparing the Philosopher's Stone, and of combining the elements without first separating them. Nevertheless, for the preparation of the true Elixir, thou needest the aid of a wise and truly learned man. Aristotle says: "Where the physicist ends, there the physician begins." Nor can we attain to true alchemy, until we begin to follow Nature, and to be guided by a knowledge of her principles. Where the study of Alchemy is rightly carried on, it is mightily advanced by Nature. But, for all that, we must not suppose that every natural substance must be useful to the alchemist. We must remember that Alchemy has a threefold aim: First, to quicken and perfect the metal, and so to digest its spirit that none of it is lost; secondly, so to digest and heat the substance in a small phial that (without the addition of anything else) the body and spirit are changed into one. The mingling of the elements is performed, not by the artist, but by thee. Thirdly, it (alchemy) proves that the process of preparing the Stone does not include any separation of the four elements (of the quicksilver and the Sun, which is called red and glorious gold). To believe that such a separation must take place is a great mistake, and contradicts the fundamental principles of philosophy.

Again, it is an undoubted fact, that every elementary substance is fed by the elements themselves. If, then, that which now forms one object is dissolved, the object as such is destroyed, the bond which held the elements together being violently broken, and each returning to that from which it was first taken. A father that begets a son must not be destroyed for that purpose; it suffices that the generating spirit shall go forth with the seed, and be conceived by the female seed, and cherished with its warmth. Such a generating spirit has power to beget an infant of the same species, as Avicenna says. Now, it is the same with pure gold, which is the true matter of the Philosophical Stone. For the father is the active principle, and must not be destroyed, or resolved into its elements, but it is sufficient for the paternal Sun (gold) to breathe its virtue and strength through the mother into the son. When the mother (who is of the earth) brings forth, the son is seen to have the father's substance.

Thus, I have learnt from thee, O Nature, that Alchemy is a true science, and that the deep red gold, which is called Sun, is the true father of the Stone or Elixir, from which this great and precious treasure proceeds; which heats, digests, and cunningly tinges (without the least diminution or corruption) the other principle of that gold, and thus brings forth so glorious a son. It is worse than useless, therefore, to meddle with the composition, or to separate the elements, which Nature has so skilfully combined in the quicksilver, and in the perfect body of the gold. All we have to do is to imitate Nature, and use the instruments with which she combines the elements, and which she uses in moulding minerals, and in giving its form to the quicksilver. If we act otherwise, wt destroy thy works, and sever the golden chain which thou hast forged. Nevertheless, we must, as Aristotle says, transmute the elements that we may obtain the object of our search.

Thus thou hast wisely led me into thy way, and hast shewn me the utter folly of my own doings. Unto thee I render the most heartfelt thanks for that thou hast delivered me from my own ignorance, and from the disgrace and ruin to which all my endless alembics, quicksilvers, aquæ fortes, dissolutions, excrements of horses, and coal fires, must at length have brought me.

In future, I will read thy book more diligently, and obey thee more implicitly. For this is the surest and safest way that a man can go, because the Art is entirely in thy hands, although, by reason of its gigantic aim, its progress must necessarily be slow. Therefore, I will lose no more time, and first begin to think about the substance, the active principle of which shall yield me most potent quicksilver. That I will enclose in a clean, air-tight phial, and under it I will place an alembic; thereupon thou wilt wait upon thine office. From the bottom of my heart I once more render unto thee the debt of unspeakable gratitude, for that thou hast deigned to visit me, and to bestow upon me so precious an inheritance. in token of my gratitude I will now do thy bidding, and let it be my ceaseless aim to attain to this most glorious Tincture of the Elements, feeling assured that with the help of the thrice great and good God, I shall succeed.

www.ingramcontent.com/pod-product-compliance
Lightning Source LLC
Chambersburg PA
CBHW071752090426
42738CB00011B/2654